DANGEROUS DISEASES

Chickenpox

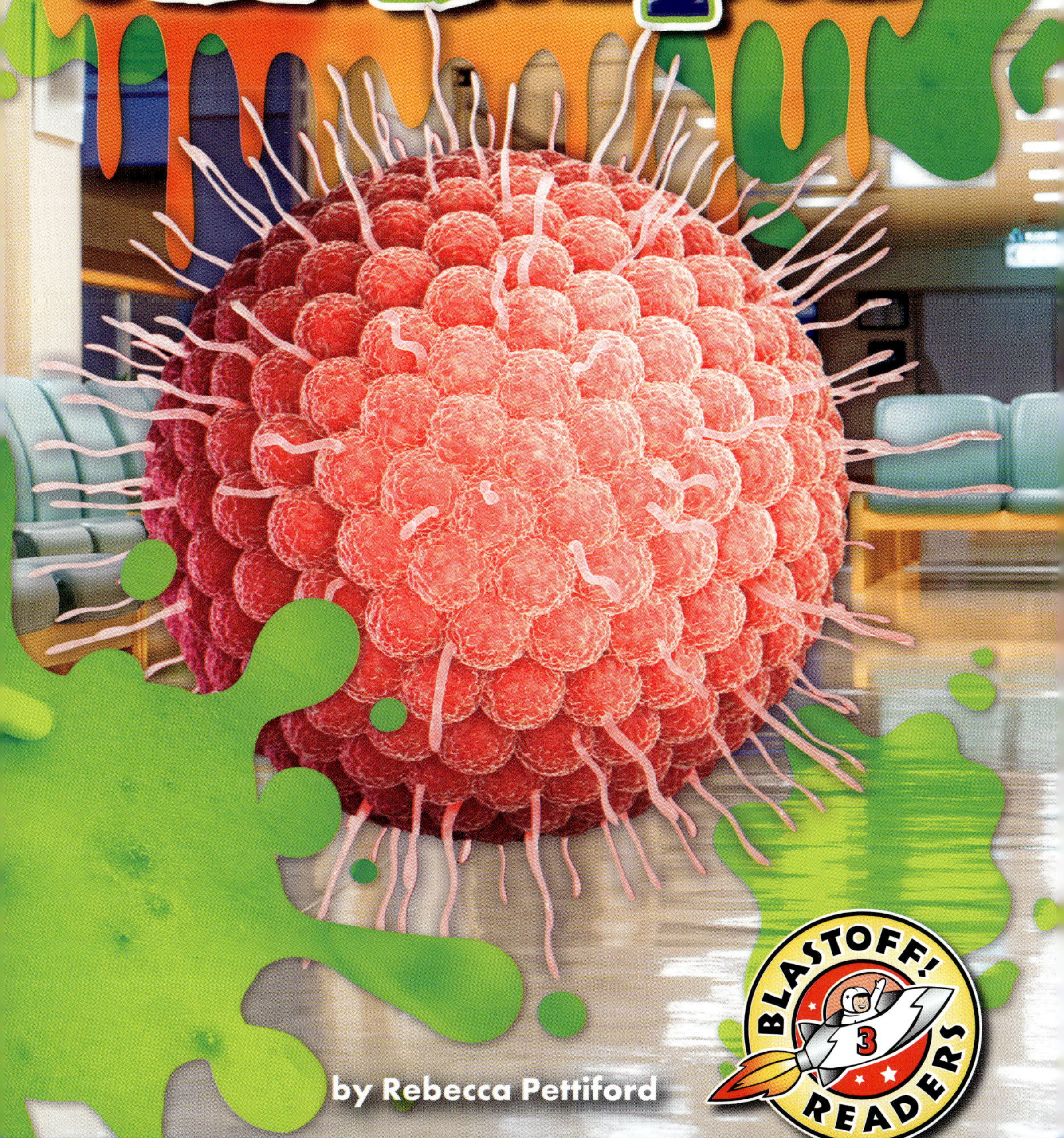

by Rebecca Pettiford

BLASTOFF! READERS, AN IMPRINT OF BELLWETHER MEDIA BY FLUTTERBEE

Blastoff! Readers are carefully developed by literacy experts to build reading stamina and move students toward fluency by combining standards-based content with developmentally appropriate text.

Level 1 provides the most support through repetition of high-frequency words, light text, predictable sentence patterns, and strong visual support.

Level 2 offers early readers a bit more challenge through varied sentences, increased text load, and text-supportive special features.

Level 3 advances early-fluent readers toward fluency through increased text load, less reliance on photos, advancing concepts, longer sentences, and more complex special features.

★ **Blastoff! Universe**

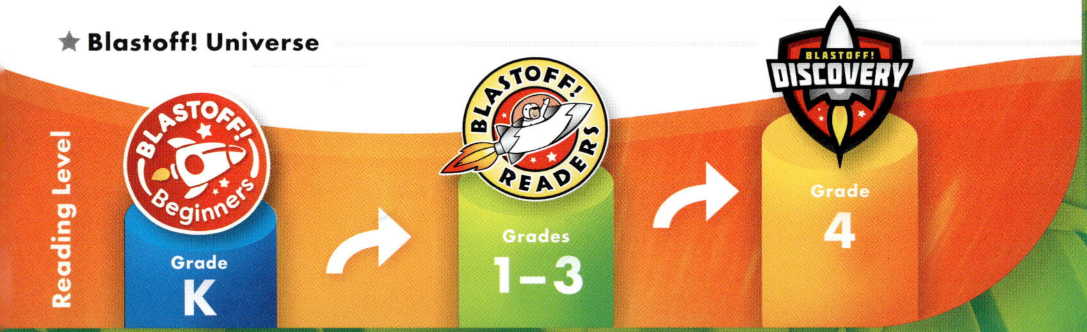

This edition first published in 2027 by Bellwether Media, Inc.

For information regarding permission, write to Bellwether Media, Inc., Attention: Permissions Department, 3500 American Blvd W, Suite 150, Bloomington, MN 55431.

Library of Congress Cataloging-in-Publication Data is available at www.loc.gov or upon request from the publisher.

ISBN: 9798898800635 (hardcover)
ISBN: 9798898801878 (ebook)

Editor: Suzane Nguyen Designer: Brittany McIntosh

Printed in the United States of America, North Mankato, MN.

Table of Contents

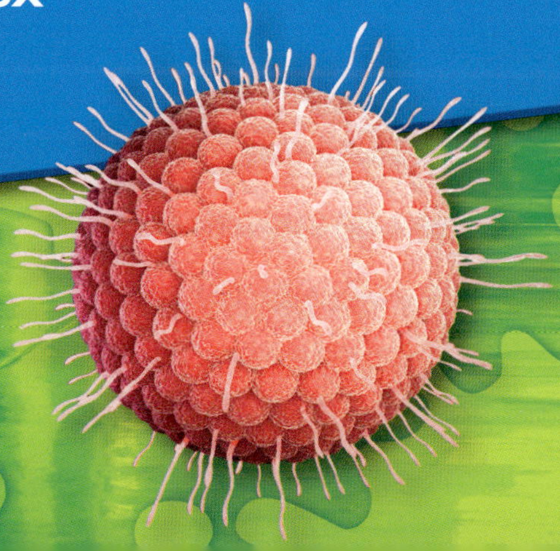

What Is Chickenpox?

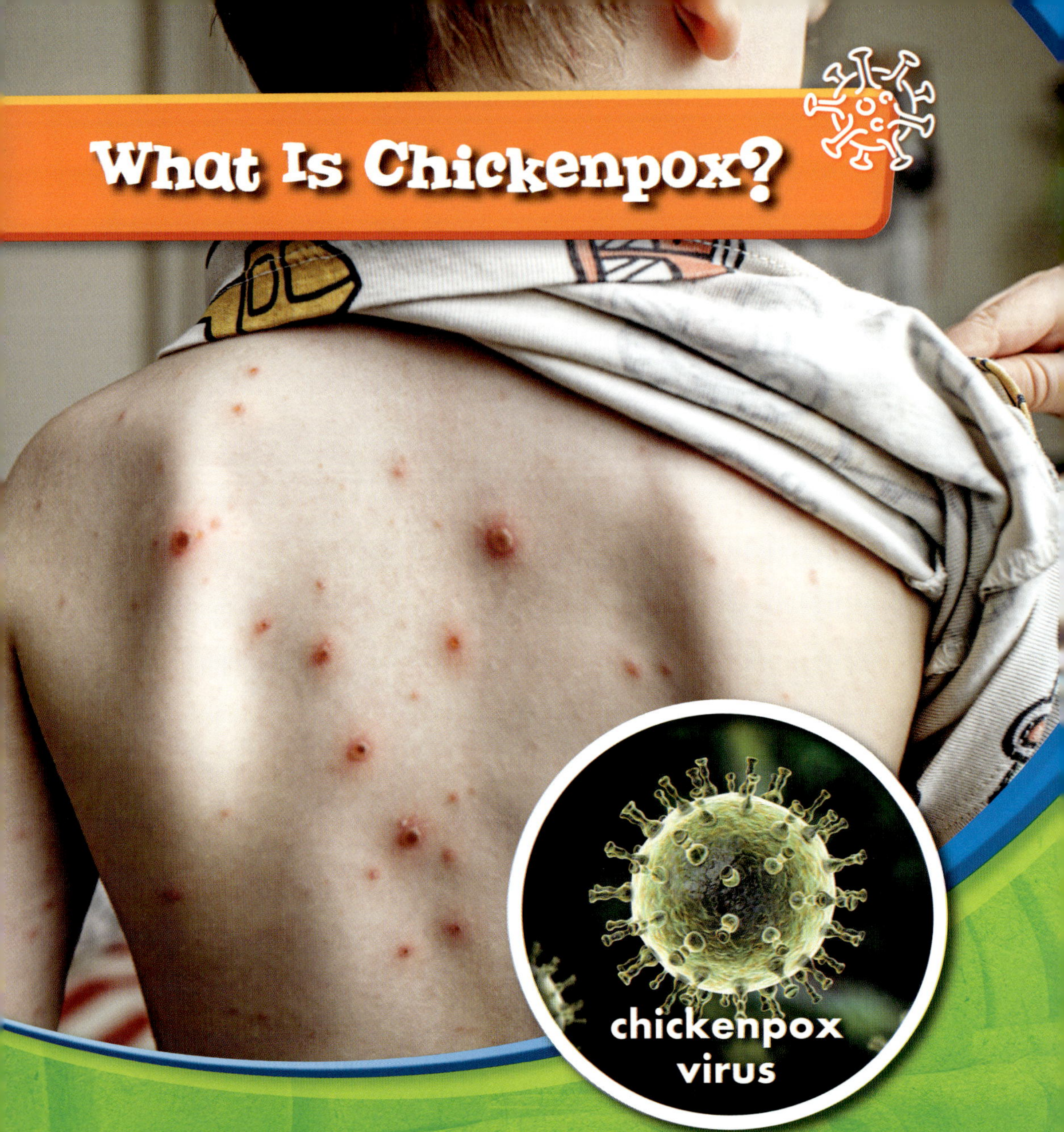

Chickenpox is a **contagious** illness. It is caused by a **virus**.

Early signs include a **fever** and headache. A **rash** appears on the face and body. It turns into **blisters**. They itch!

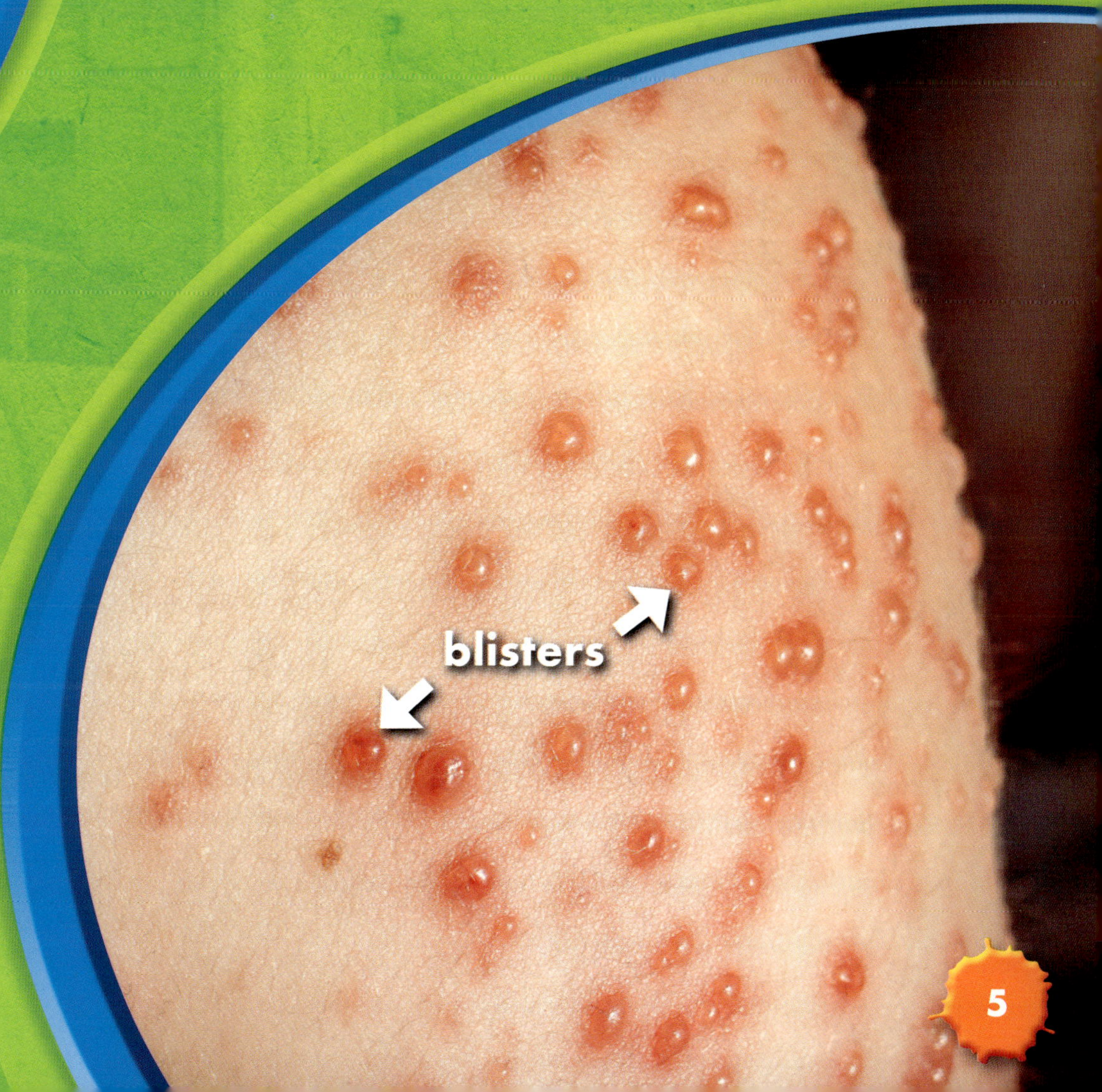

The United States once had more than four million cases of chickenpox each year. Today, there is a **vaccine**.

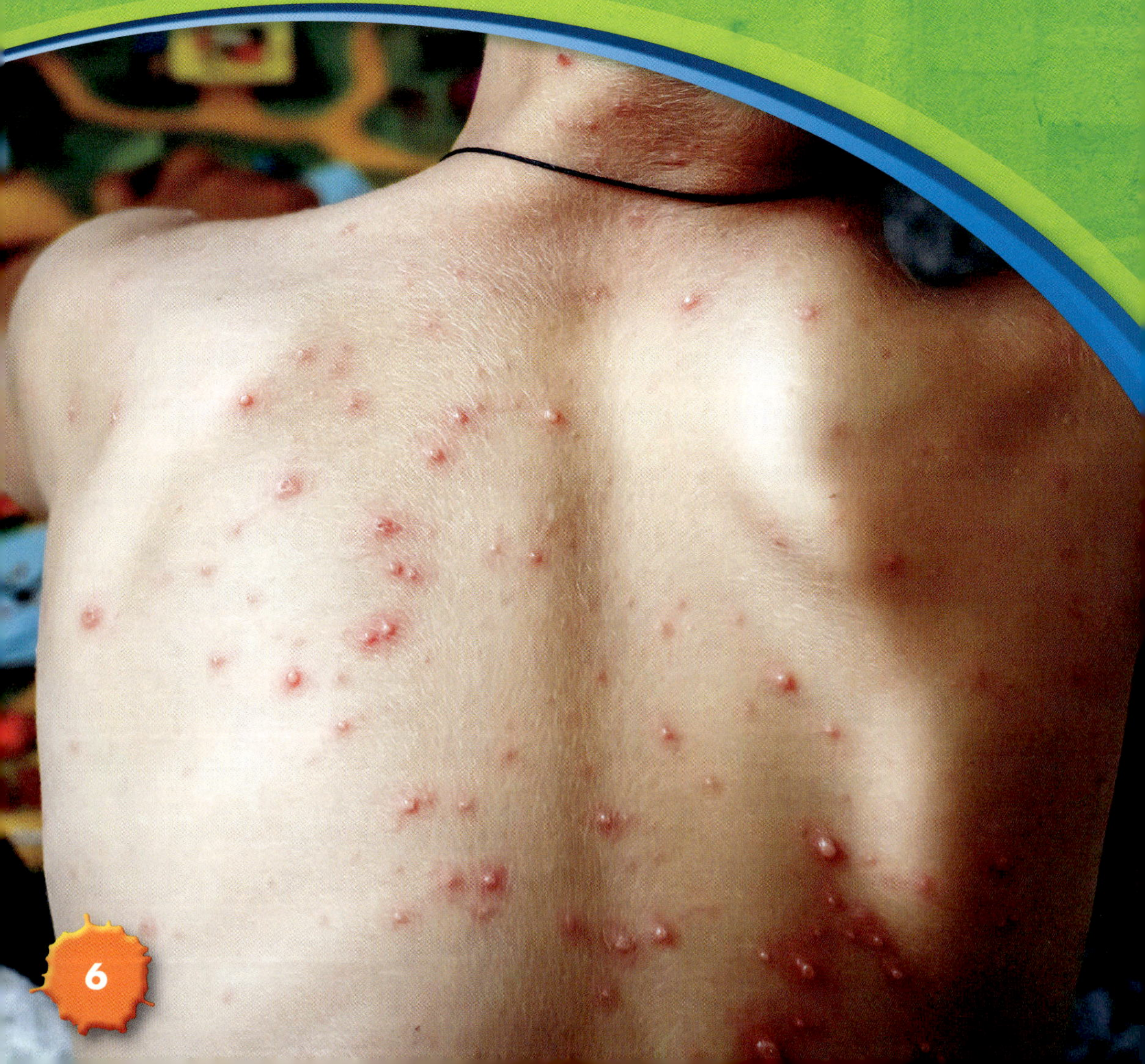

Long-term Effects

People who have had chickenpox as children can have shingles as adults. Signs include a rash and burning feeling on the skin.

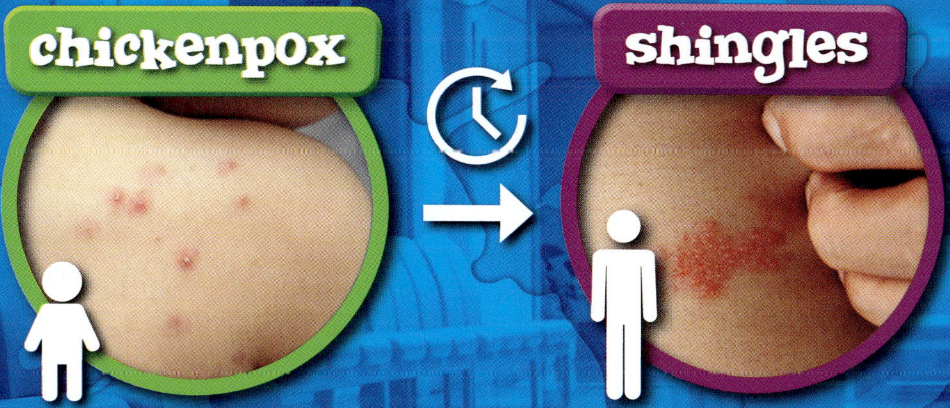

Each year, fewer than 150,000 people get chickenpox. Fewer than 30 of them die from it.

History of Chickenpox

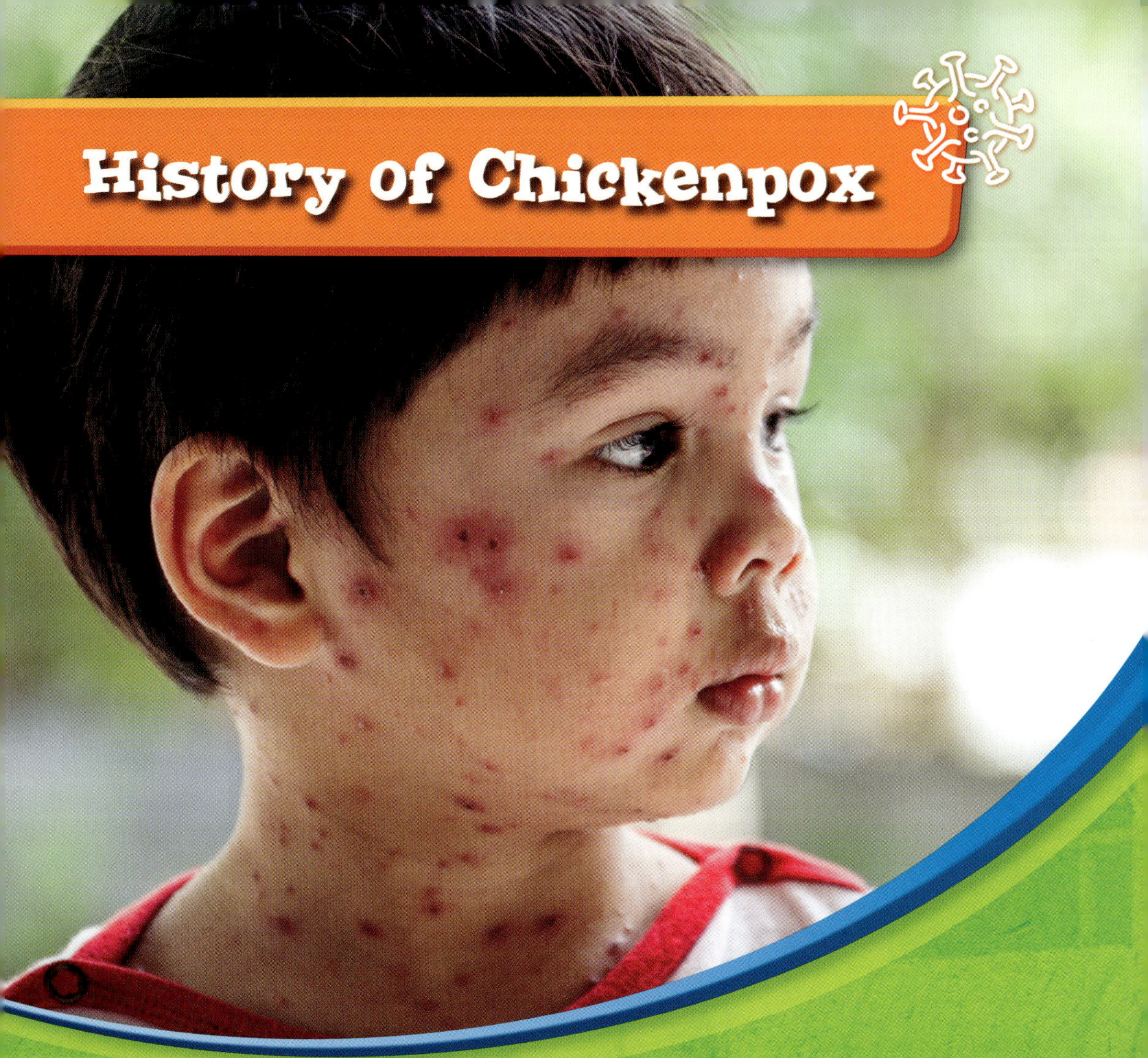

Chickenpox has been around for a long time. Many places around the world have records of chickenpox.

In the 1700s, an English doctor wrote an important work about chickenpox.

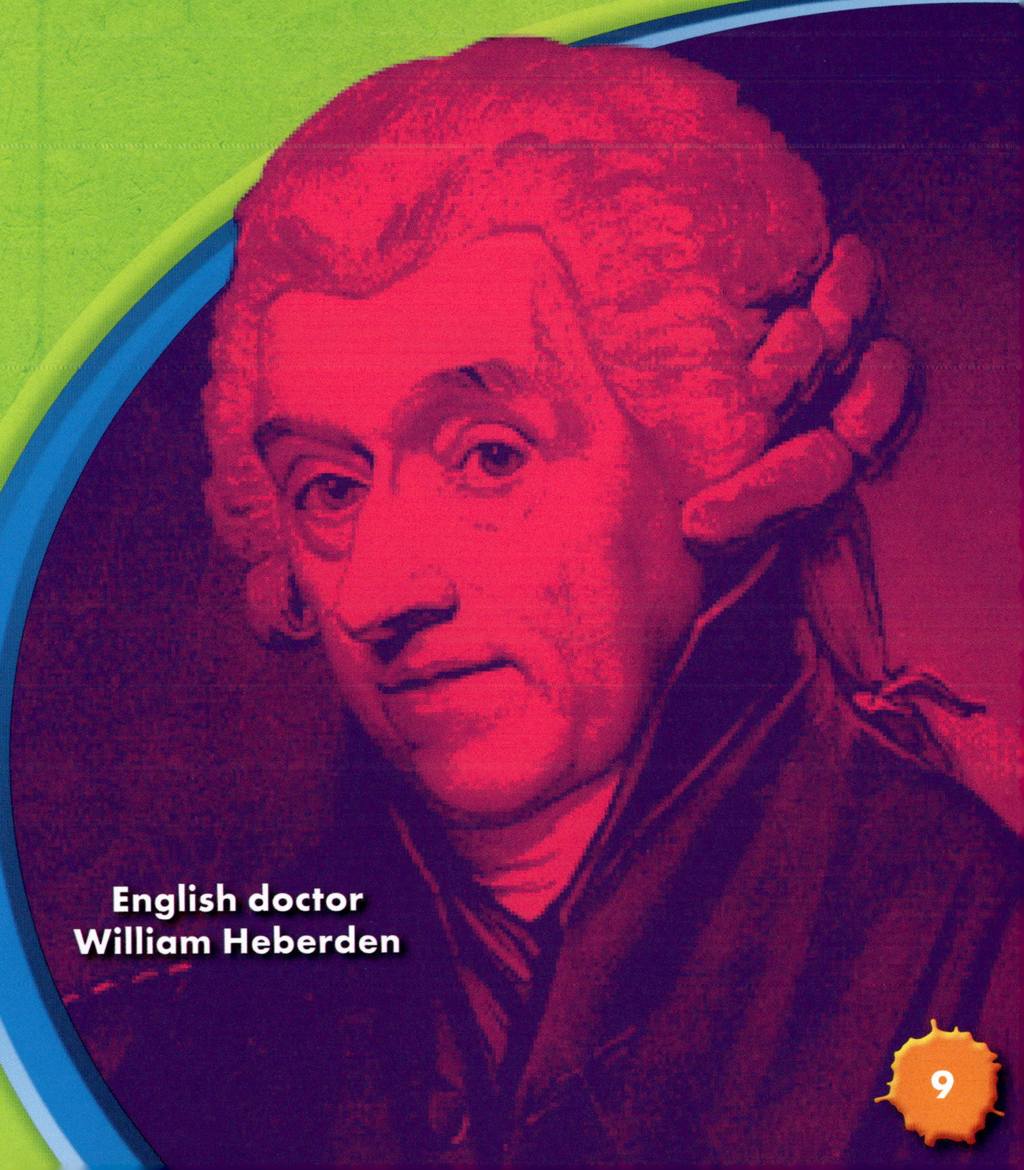

English doctor William Heberden

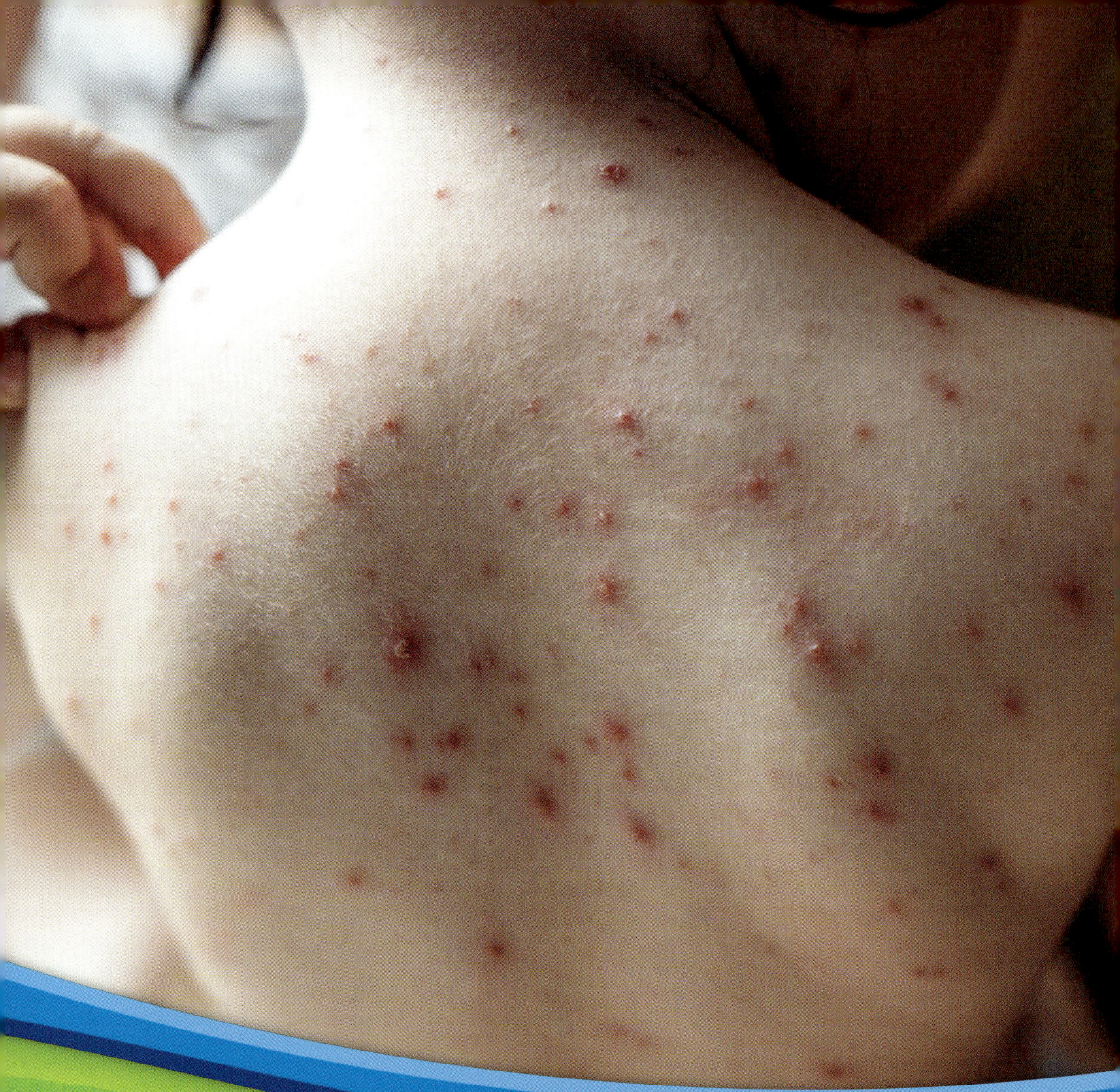

In 1954, scientists **isolated** the virus. They learned the virus causes chickenpox and shingles.

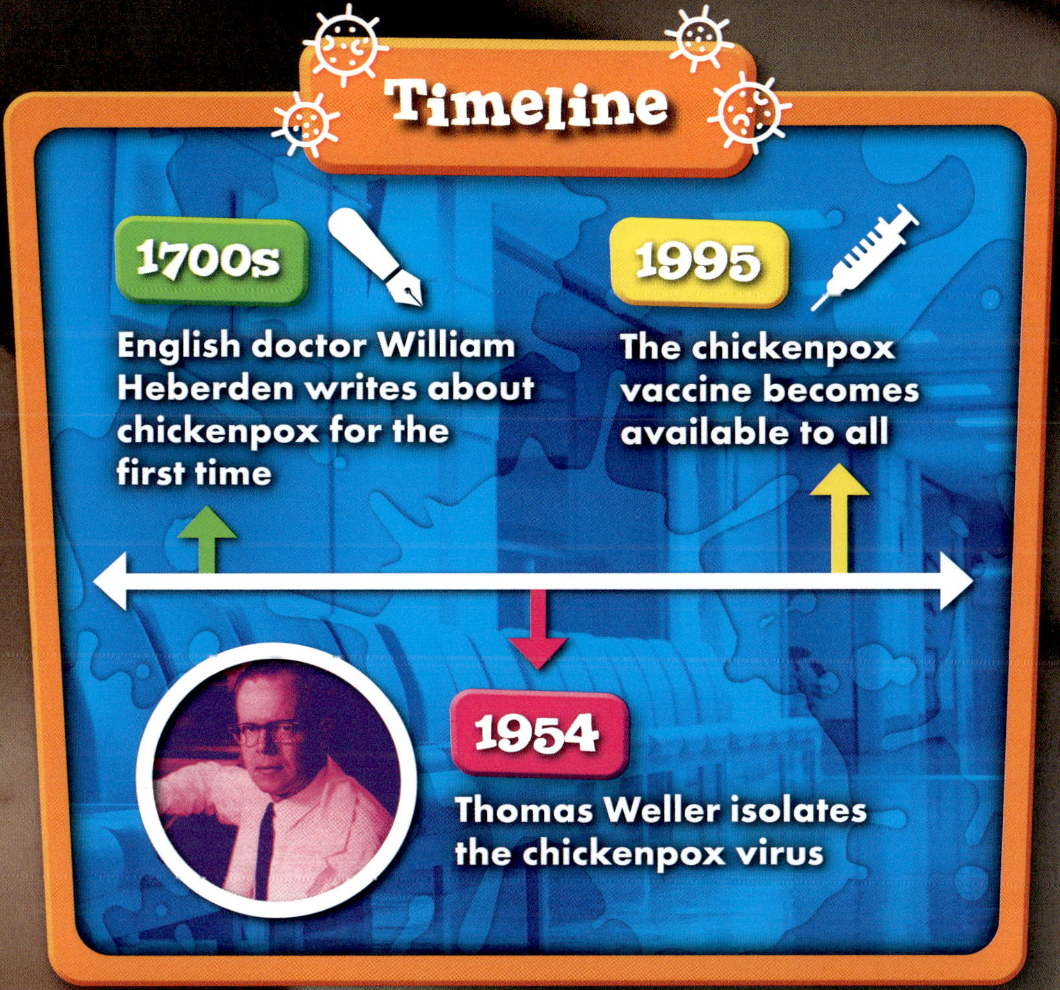

The first chickenpox vaccine was made in Japan in 1974. In 1995, the vaccine became available to all.

How Does Chickenpox Spread?

Chickenpox spreads through droplets in the air. This happens when a person with chickenpox coughs or sneezes.

Some people are not **immune**. They breathe in the droplets. They get chickenpox.

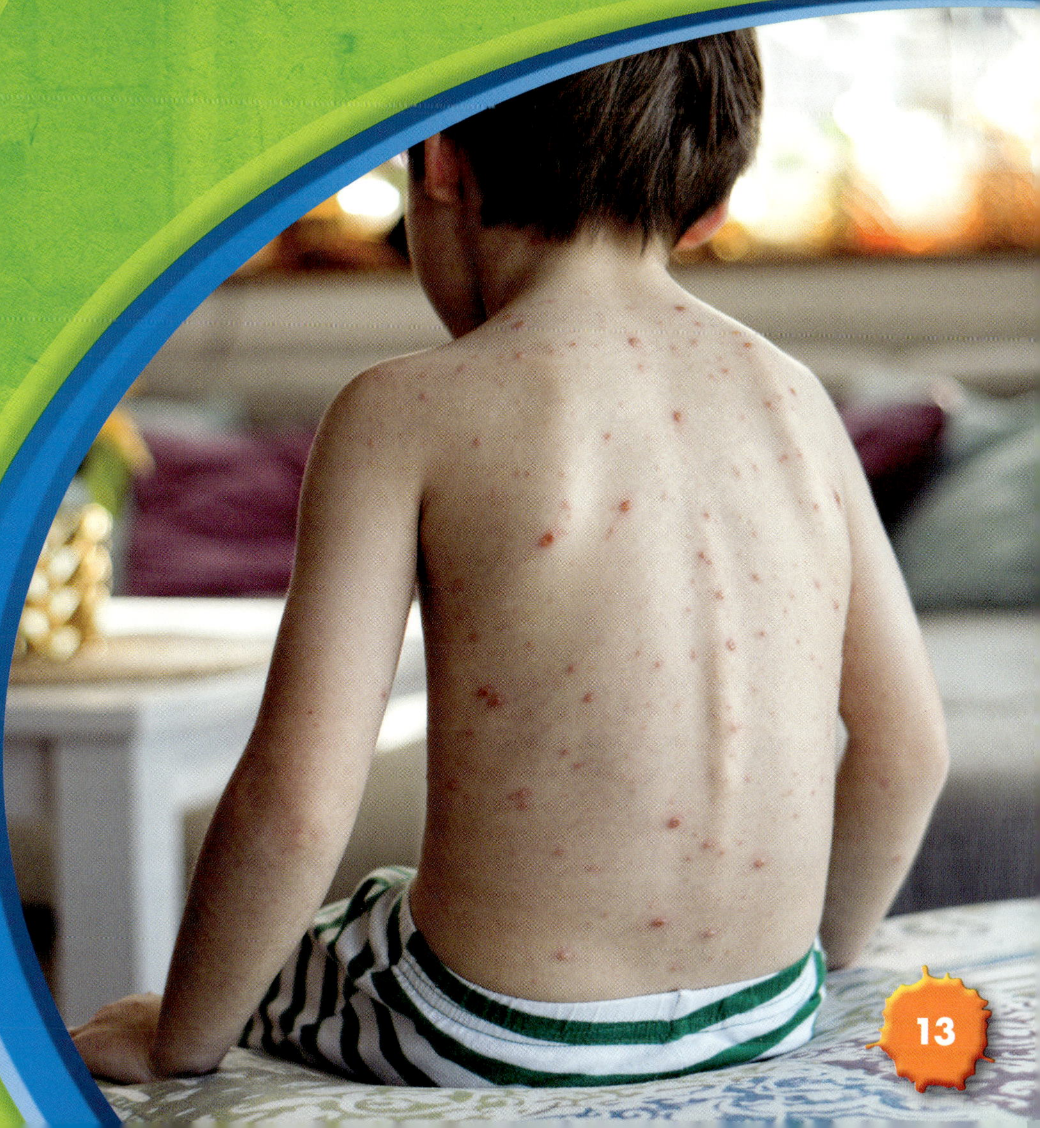

Chickenpox can spread through touch. Blisters have **fluid**. A person can catch chickenpox from touching it.

After around seven days, the blisters turn into **scabs**. Scabs do not spread chickenpox.

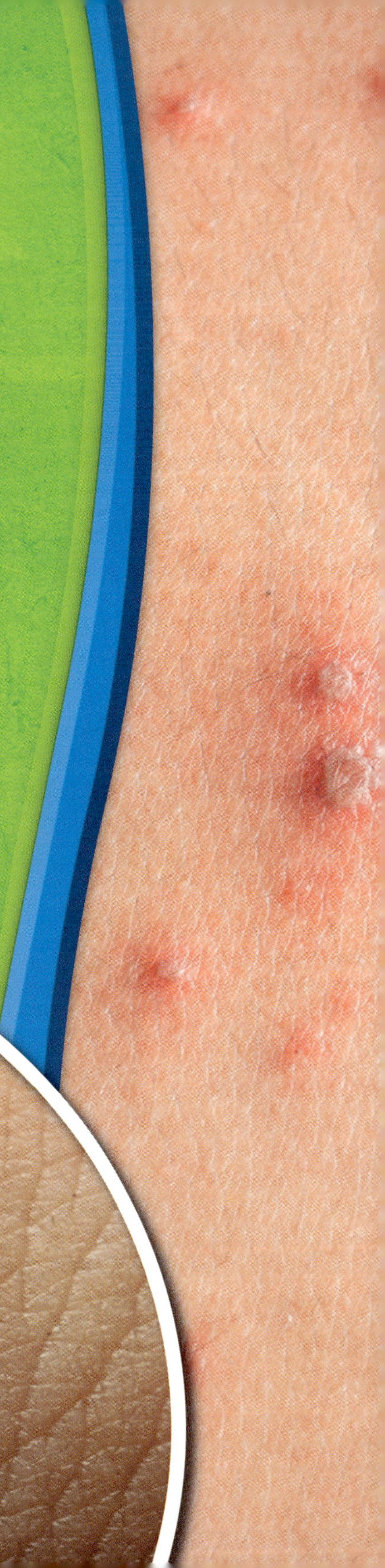

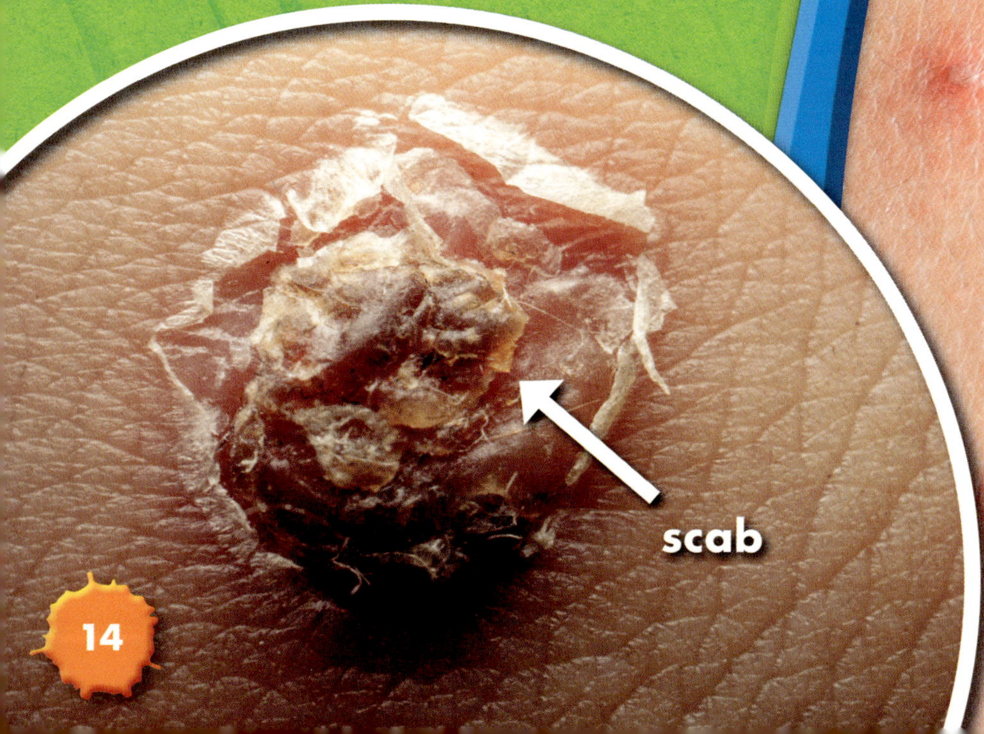

How Chickenpox Spreads

By Air

1

Someone coughs or sneezes.

2

Droplets in the air enter a person's mouth or nose.

3

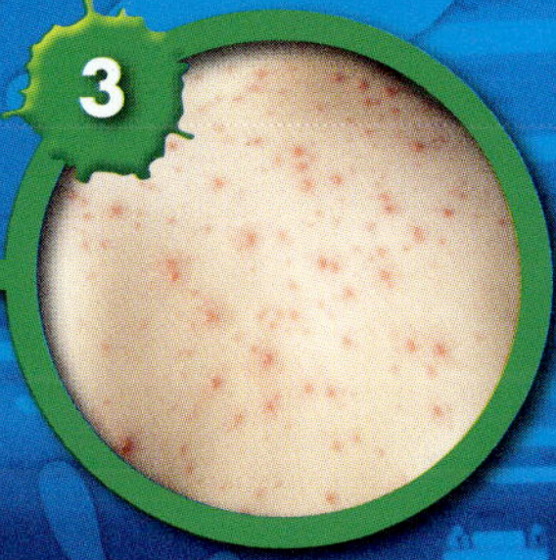

Person gets chickenpox.

By Touch

1

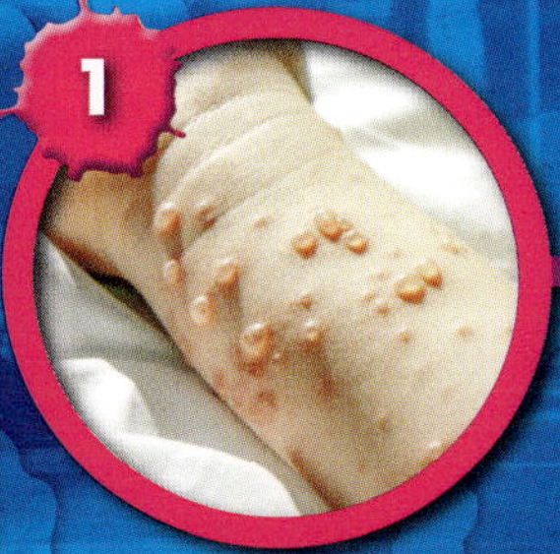

Fluid comes from blisters.

2

Person touches the fluid.

3

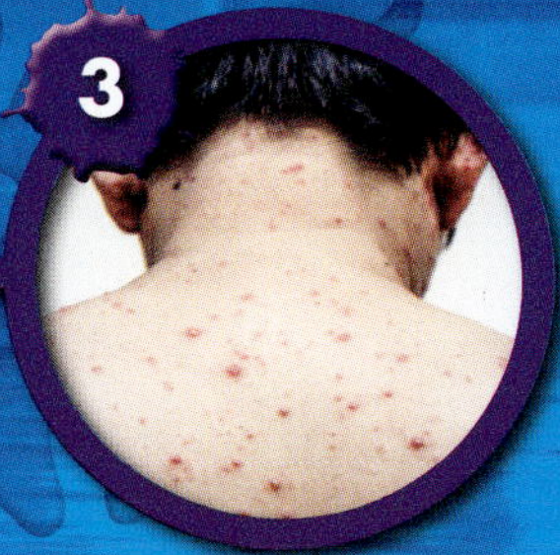

Person gets chickenpox.

Prevention and Treatment

The chickenpox vaccine is the best way to stay well. It gives people a weak form of the virus. Their **immune system** makes **antibodies**.

People keep away from those with chickenpox to stay healthy.

Healing Hero

Name

Doctor Michiaki Takahashi

Year Helped

1974

How He Helped

Made the first chickenpox vaccine

Chickenpox can take up to three weeks to appear. It can take around two weeks to get better.

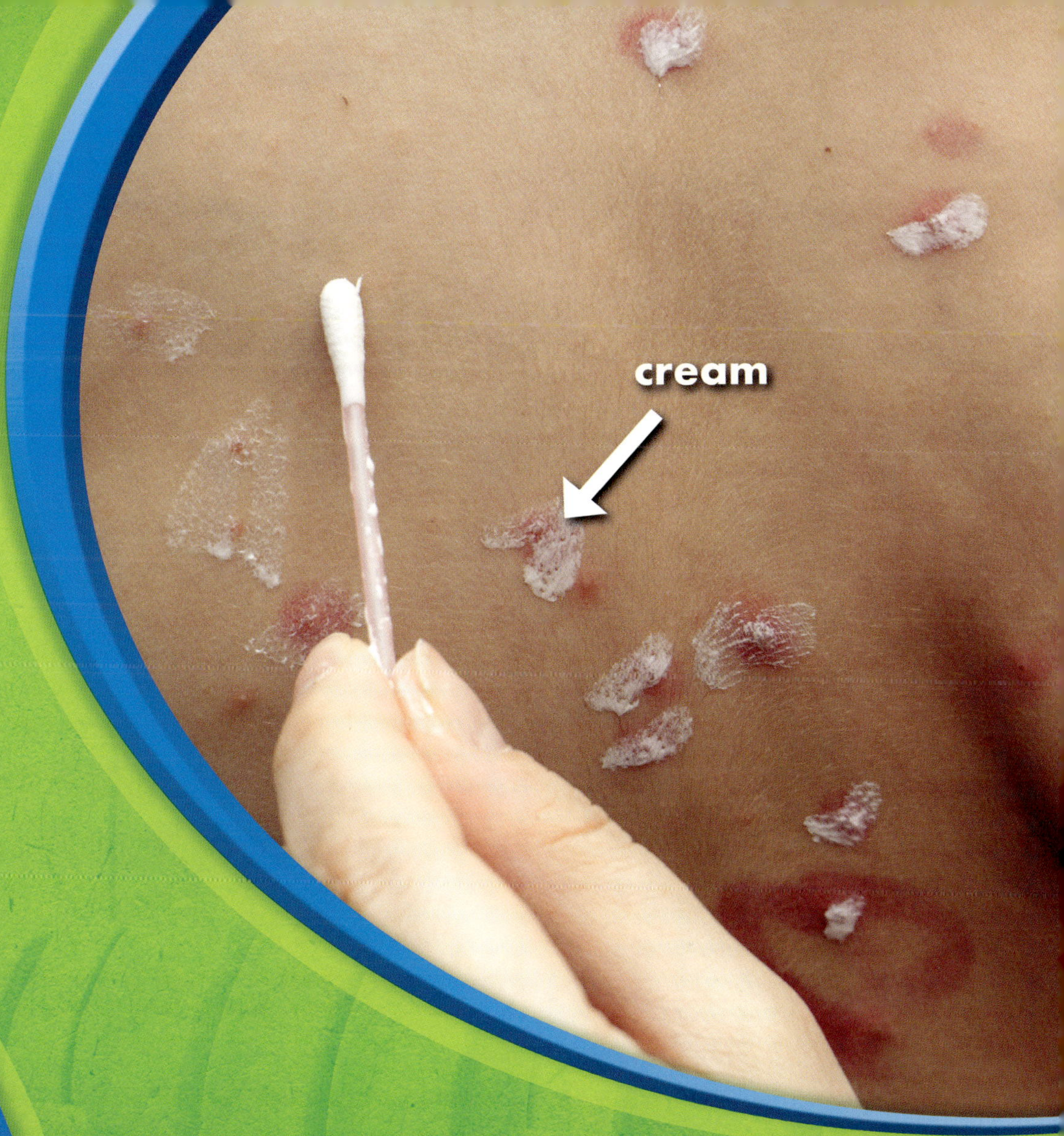

People take **medicine** for fever. Skin creams calm blisters and itching.

Before the vaccine, chickenpox was common in children. Few adults got it.

Most people who get chickenpox will be immune to it for the rest of their lives!

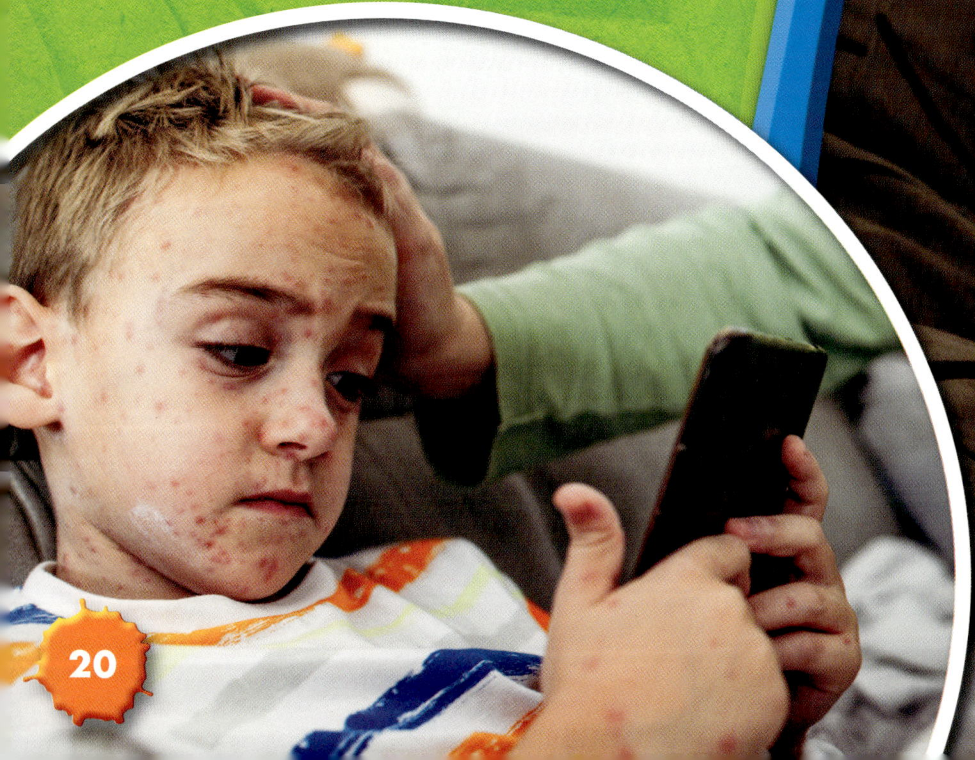

Glossary

antibodies–materials that the body makes to fight illnesses

blisters–large, round bumps on the skin that are filled with liquid

contagious–able to spread

fever–a higher-than-normal body temperature

fluid–a liquid or a material that can flow

immune–unable to get sick easily

immune system–the system that protects the body from illnesses

isolated–separated from its surroundings

medicine–something taken to treat an illness

rash–an area of itchy, red spots on the skin

scabs–hard, dry layers that form over blisters or cuts

vaccine–a substance that is put into the body to help fight off an illness; a person who has gotten the vaccine is vaccinated.

virus–a tiny living thing that causes illness in people, animals, and plants

To Learn More

AT THE LIBRARY

LaRocca, Rajani. *A Vaccine Is Like a Memory.* New York, N.Y.: Little Bee Books, 2023.

Troupe, Thomas Kingsley. *What Would Happen If You Never Got Vaccines?* Mankato, Minn.: Amicus Learning, 2024.

Schuh, Mari. *Iker's Incredible Immune System.* Minneapolis, Minn.: Jump!, 2022.

ON THE WEB

FACTSURFER

Factsurfer.com gives you a safe, fun way to find more information.

1. Go to www.factsurfer.com.
2. Enter "chickenpox" into the search box and click .
3. Select your book cover to see a list of related content.

Index

The images in this book are reproduced through the courtesy of: Tatiana Shepeleva, front cover (hero), p. 3; Vitalis83, front cover (splatter left), pp. 7 (left), 19; sergiophoto, front cover (splatter right); Princess_Anmitsu, front cover (back); Hadrian, p. 4; Kateryna Kon, p. 4 (inset); almo Creative, pp. 5, 14 (by touch 1); Severyn Bogdana, p. 6; Suriyawut Suriya, p. 7 (right); thanongsak kongtong, p. 8; Wellcome Trust/ Wikipedia, p. 9; Mixmike, pp. 10-11; Science History Images/ Alamy Stock Photo, p. 11; jarenwicklund, p. 12; domin_domin, p. 13; Daniel, p. 14; Charoen Krung Photography, pp. 14-15; Pixel-Shot, pp. 14 (by air 1, by touch 2), 18; Hakase_420, p. 14 (by air 2); Fhotodrozd, p. 14 (by air 3); 9Gawin, p. 14 (by touch 3); WONG SZE FEI, p. 16; Ko Sasaki, p. 17; SBDIGIT, p. 20; Troyan, p. 21.